Canadian Art: Vital Decades

The McMichael Conservation Collection □ With an introduction by Paul Duval

Clarke, Irwin & Company Limited TORONTO, VANCOUVER 1970

Through the years, many will
receive joy and knowledge
because a few have given
treasured possessions to the
Collection.

©1970 McMichael Conservation Collection
ISBN 0 7720 0045 X
Printed in Canada

front cover: Tom Thomson
Ragged Pine, 1916
8½ x 10½

The
McMichael
Conservation Collection
of Art

KLEINBURG · ONTARIO

PAUL DUVAL

The most interesting personal art collections in the world have been born of a compelling enthusiasm for a particular period or kind of art. Material for such collections may be the work of one painter, one nation or one school of artists.

The enthusiasm that founded the McMichael Conservation Collection was triggered by the art of a legendary Canadian, Tom Thomson and those Group of Seven painters who shared his devotion to our native landscape.

Robert and Signe McMichael were attuned since childhood to the grandeur and scale of the Canadian earth. Long before they were married, they separately came to know the tundra, forests and streams of the wilderness. Signe McMichael arrived from Europe with her Danish parents when she was six years old, and spent her formative years on the family's farm in the Peace River district of the far northwest. Bob though born in Toronto, had vivid recollections of many summer trips which included Algonquin Park and the Timagami area of Northern Ontario. For both of the McMichaels, love of art has long run in tandem with their affection for the land which first nurtured their visual experience.

Born to a generation that inherited the works of Tom Thomson and the Group of Seven almost wet from the easel, the McMichaels first came to enjoy art from the reproductions of Thomson's West Wind and Jack Pine in their school textbooks. For both of them, Thomson has remained a special favorite among artists.

Although a Thomson painting was not their first purchase (they had earlier bought a canvas by Tom Wood and a Montreal River sketch by Lawren Harris), the McMichael's acquisition of Thomson's Pine Island sketch in 1953 started them earnestly on the road to the magnificent public collection of today. Only a year later, in 1954, they moved into the unfinished first stage of what is today the McMichael Conservation Collection gallery. It was erected on ten acres of land purchased in the winter of 1952 on the outskirts of Kleinburg, then a village of about two hundred persons.

When they first bought the site of their country home only twenty miles from Toronto, Bob and Signe could hardly imagine where their love of the outdoors and art would eventually lead them. Certainly, a large collection of Canadian treasures had not yet been envisioned. There were enough problems paying for and completing their new home. They had decided to build it from pioneer Ontario materials, stone and square-hewn logs. Two patient years had been spent searching out old barns from whose century-old timbers their first four room home was constructed. Bob and Signe were fortunate to locate expert local craftsmen, under the supervision of A. W. Bayliss to fit the nine-inch thick logs and local rock to shape. The same craftsmen have since continued to fashion each addition to the gallery-home and the building is thus as much a harmonious unit as the collection of art it houses.

When the first stage of the McMichael house was completed, it was an L-shaped structure of four rooms, one of them a vast living room 42 x 22 feet, centred by a huge fireplace. The young couple called their new home Tapawingo, the Indian word for Place of Joy, and in November, 1954, they settled in to enjoy the isolation and beauty of their ten-acre country estate, with its magnificent views of first growth forest, sloping hills and a constantly changing parade of animal and bird life.

The natural beauty that surrounded Tapawingo was soon to be balanced within its walls by beauty created by man. When the McMichaels bought their first Harris and Thomson sketches in 1953 on the installment plan they became, as Bob stated it, "hooked on Canadian art". They visualized the walls of Tapawingo decorated with paintings by Thomson, the Group of Seven and their great contemporaries, Emily Carr and David Milne. Every dollar that could be spared from the expanding McMichael business interests went toward buying paintings and by 1960 almost fifty canvases and sketches had been acquired.

It was at this point that friends and acquaintances began to bring visitors to see the growing collection in its unique natural setting. They would sit enjoying the McMichael's hospitality, a Group of Seven canvas sharing their line of sight with the view through a panoramic window. During these visits, the subjects of painting and collecting were often foremost.

Frequent visitors to Tapawingo were many of the famed Group of Seven members themselves. A. Y. Jackson, A. J. Casson, F. H. Varley and J. E. H. MacDonald's artist-son, Thoreau, became firm friends and assisted the McMichaels in many ways, as did the painter Yvonne Housser. As these meetings and talks continued, Bob and Signe began to visualize Tapawingo as a continuing "Place of Joy" for anyone who wished to share it. They started to draw up plans for a gallery which would be given to the people of Canada, a gallery where paintings by Tom Thomson, the Group of Seven and their contemporaries would be on permanent view.

The functions of a home were gradually superseded at Tapawingo by the needs of a gallery. The next two stages in its construction, completed in 1963 and 1966, were designed

primarily as exhibition areas for the effective display of paintings.

In 1962, a unique annex was added to Tapawingo, with the acquisition of the shack in which Tom Thomson had lived and painted in downtown Toronto's Rosedale Valley. Thomson had painted the West Wind and other famous masterpieces in this small wooden structure located behind the Group of Seven's Studio Building. Its removal, plank by plank, and re-erection on the McMichael property has made it possible to preserve the historic building and convert it into an exhibition area for objects and material relating to Thomson's life and times.

Its walls are decorated with paintings done originally for the walls of the shack by the Group and others, along with a series of witty contemporary impressions of the Group members by Arthur Lismer. Among other items on display are Thomson's own easel and palette.

Tapawingo, which had begun as a cherished and very private retreat for two people, was rapidly becoming a public shrine for lovers of Canadian art.

As early as 1962, thousands of visitors were coming to see the McMichael collection. Individuals and groups would appear at the door unannounced to see the collection about which they had read or heard. Signe and Bob would accommodate the unexpected callers as much as possible. They considered any inconvenience to themselves compensated by the eagerness of their visitors for Canadian art. Soon, school classes, community clubs, convention groups and other organizations were making appointments to see Tapawingo. By 1964, the annual number of visitors had increased to more than eleven thousand.

One of those 1964 visitors was the Honourable John Robarts, Prime Minister of Ontario. A keen conservationist and enthusiast for Canadian art, Mr. Robarts was deeply impressed by what the McMichaels had achieved. Subsequent visits between the Prime Minister, members of his staff and the McMichaels brought about the realization of Bob and Signe's most cherished ambition. Tapawingo and a surrounding 600 acres was to become a public institution administered jointly by the Government of Ontario and the Metropolitan Toronto and Region Conservation Authority.

The home and collection which had given the young couple so much pleasure was now to be given to as many people as wished to come and enjoy it, for as long as man can foresee. It was only one short decade since Bob and Signe had first moved into their unfinished home.

On November 18th, 1965, an agreement was signed between Prime Minister John Robarts, for the Government of Ontario, and the McMichaels, creating the McMichael Conservation Collection of Art, and the McMichael Conservation Area as a gift to Canada, in the Right of the Province of Ontario. By this time the McMichael Collection had grown to over two hundred important works. The terms of this document stipulate that the Province of Ontario guarantees to maintain the grounds, buildings and collection into perpetuity and add such facilities as would be deemed necessary for ever increasing attendance. The 600 acres of the McMichael Conservation Area and the 30 acres that embrace the Collection would be tended and protected by Government staffs. Bob and Signe McMichael would remain at Tapawingo as unpaid curators and would supervise the growing size and quality of the now-public collection.

During its first six months as a public institution, more than forty thousand people came to see the collection between May and November. They arrived, not only from surrounding towns and cities, but from as far away as the Pacific Coast and deep into the United States. Articles about the collection in national and international publications brought it to the notice of millions of potential visitors.

By 1967, the Collection numbered two hundred and eighty-seven canvases, sketches and drawings. The great majority of these were amassed personally by the McMichaels, but they proudly made it known that many of the paintings and sketches were gifts of other Canadian collectors who admired what was evolving in Kleinburg.

These early donors are many and are separately noted elsewhere in this book, but special mention should be made of a few, such as the late Dr. Arnold Mason. A friend to several members of the Group of Seven, Dr. Mason paved the way for the acquisition of such masterpieces as J. E. H. MacDonald's *Leaves in the Brook* and F. H. Varley's *Mountain Portage*. Robert A. Laidlaw, a distinguished collector and close friend of many Group members, presented twenty-six paintings to the McMichaels, including nine brilliant Tom Thomson sketches. Norah de Pencier of Owen Sound, an early supporter of the Group, gave among other works, a major A. Y. Jackson canvas, *Grey Day, Laurentians,* and Emily Carr's dramatic *Shoreline*. Yvonne Housser added noteable items, including Mrs. Housser's outstanding Lawren Harris, *Lake Superior Island*.

"These gifts have been one of the biggest joys of our entire art experience", Bob McMichael stated. "It is not the paintings themselves, wonderful and welcome though they are, but, even more, the reassurance to Signe and me that our ideas and aims are shared and supported by distinguished Canadians who have been experiencing and collecting art much longer than we have."

If there could be said to be a cornerstone of the Collection it would almost certainly be the group of fifty-five paintings and drawings by Tom Thomson.

The art of Tom Thomson has always had a special meaning for the McMichaels, as it has for most Canadians. The magic of his style, his close identification with the wilderness and his legendary life have put him to the forefront as a symbol of an art that is totally national. The name Tom Thomson is synonymous with the search for a native art expression. The selection from his production in the McMichael Collection allows one to see his search through its total evolution.

Although he was only forty when he drowned mysteriously in Algonquin Park's Canoe Lake, Thomson achieved an astonishing body of work. His large canvases are few, but his small oil panels number into hundreds. He managed to produce these while spending much of his time as a guide and fire ranger.

Thomson's finest and most characteristic art was compressed into a brief period of three years, from 1914 until the summer of his death in 1917. Thomson started very slowly as an artist. He was doing dull, imitative, and not very accomplished drawings of figures and landscapes well into his thirties, an age when most artists have already achieved a personal authority of style. In the McMichael Collection examples of these early founderings are available to provide valuable comparisons with the achievements of his last years. It is difficult to believe that these earlier pieces were done only a few years before Thomson first visited Algonquin Park, and became, virtually overnight a totally equipped master of landscape painting.

In the little *Fairy Lake* sketch of 1910, Thomson gives some inkling of his ability to capture mood, but it is still a painting dictated by the subject: the artist is not in command. In the canvas *Afternoon, Algonquin Park,* Thomson begins to find his true style —that combination of exact observation and spirited execution that was his own. Then in such 1915 sketches as *Burned Over Land* and *The Log Flume,* he breaks into the radiant color and commanding brushwork that led to the climactic intensity of his last 1917 studies.

Born in Claremont, Ontario in 1877, Tom Thomson spent his boyhood in Leith, near Owen Sound. He wandered briefly to Seattle, settled in Toronto as a commercial artist, but found his spiritual and creative home in Algonquin Park. Today, in the McMichael Collection and its natural surroundings, with his shack close by, Tom Thomson has found a different sort of home, where millions in the future will be able to see our land through his eyes.

Many of the artists with whom Thomson painted were later to band together as the Group of Seven, a body which changed membership occasionally, but kept substantially the same core of adherents. The first exhibition of the Group was held at the Art Gallery of Toronto in 1920. The seven founding members were Franklin Carmichael, Lawren Harris, A. Y. Jackson, Frank (later Franz) Johnston, Arthur Lismer, J. E .H. MacDonald and Frederick H. Varley. Johnston resigned from the Group in 1922, and additional members, A. J. Casson, Edwin Holgate and LeMoine FitzGerald were added in 1926, 1931 and 1932 respectively.

The first Group of Seven work bought by the McMichaels was Lawren Harris' sketch, *Montreal River*. Unknowingly they had paid tribute in their first purchase to the man who was the driving force behind the formation of the Group of Seven.

Lawren Harris was born in Brantford, Ontario, in 1885 to a family which had helped establish an industrial empire. He was able to gain some support for his fellow painters through his connections at many levels of society.

In 1913, Harris built, in partnership with art patron Dr. James MacCallum, the famed Studio Building in Toronto, where most of those destined to form the Group of Seven were to work at some time or another. Tom Thomson occasionally shared a studio with A. Y. Jackson, but mostly worked in the shack on the Studio Building property. Franklin Carmichael, J. E. H. MacDonald, Arthur Lismer, and Harris himself, all had studios there and created most of their major works within its walls.

Apart from his lifetime efforts on behalf of other artists, Lawren Harris achieved a large body of paintings ranging over his career from impressionism to pure abstraction. Harris was at once the most intellectual and experimental of the Group members.

Over fifty examples by Harris in the McMichael Collection touch upon most of his creative phases from 1910 through the twenties. The collection is especially rich in sketches from the brilliantly colored Algoma period of 1918-1921, but also includes a number of noteable examples from the mid and late twenties, among them the starkly dramatic compositions *Lake Superior Island* and *The Ice House.*

A magnificent canvas given by R. S. McLaughlin is *Pic Island*, one of Harris' masterpieces. Hardly less important is the brooding large composition, *Mountains and Lake of 1929*. Six important mountain and arctic Harris panels were presented to the collection; three by the late Mrs. Lawren Harris and three by Mrs. Chester Harris.

Of all Canadian artists, none has become such a national institution as Alexander Young Jackson. During his painting career, A. Y. Jackson probably became familiar with more square miles of Canadian earth than any other man.

Bylot Island. 1927   A. Y. Jackson

He travelled far from Montreal where he was born in 1882, and sketched from the Maritimes to the Pacific, with regular forays into the Northwest Territories and the Arctic. His enthusiasm for painting reached beyond his own creative efforts, embracing the instruction of art as a guest teacher in all parts of the nation. He had boundless enthusiasm for such endeavors as the McMichael Conservation Collection. From virtually its beginning, Jackson was intimately involved in the building of the Collection. Through frequent visits to Tapawingo during which he gave sage and unselfish assistance, A. Y. became virtual curator emeritus of the McMichael Collection.

Among paintings and drawing by Jackson in the McMichael Collection is the monumental *First Snow*, *Algoma*,

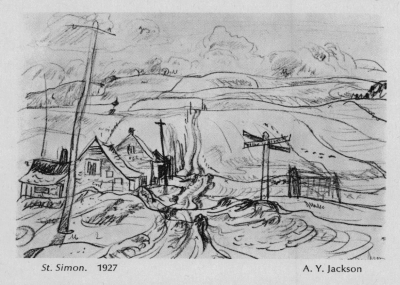

St. Simon. 1927   A. Y. Jackson

rated by the artist himself as perhaps his finest canvas. Certainly, this painting, a gift from Percy Hilborn, must be included among Jackson's highest achievements. Ranking hardly less important in any serious estimate of this artist's career, are many other canvases in the collection. The McMichael Collection is particularly rich in Jackson oil panels and drawings showing the full range of his talents. They include every period from his early European studies of Bruges to vigorous sketches of all parts of Canada. Two singular, if uncharacteristic, works are a figure study of a woman, and a portrait of Jackson's aunt's parlour painted in 1910.

In the forming of the group of works by J. E. H. MacDonald, the McMichaels have been fortunate in having the assistance

and advice of the artist's son, Thoreau. With his aid, the Collection has amassed an unrivalled selection of J. E. H. MacDonald sketches. His small oil panels are the most carefully designed sketches made by any member of the Group. His outstanding abilities as a designer, which he passed on so well to his younger colleague Tom Thomson, make almost every MacDonald sketch as complete as most major landscape canvases. A visitor has only to compare the small 8½ x 10½ inch study for *Leaves in the Brook* with the 21 x 26 inch larger version hanging nearby to see how little MacDonald left out of his on-the-spot notes.

It would be impossible to select any few favorites from the more than sixty paintings by MacDonald on view here: together, they offer a complete survey of this great Canadian artist's achievement.

Frederick H. Varley was not a prolific artist, and when the McMichaels first began to collect, fine examples of his work were exceedingly difficult to locate. Despite this handicap, the collection at Kleinburg included fifteen Varley paintings and drawings by 1967. Since then, through gifts and bequests, the number has increased to where Varley is now well represented by outstanding works. One of the most important of these remains *Mountain Portage*, a prime work of 1925, and one of the earliest to be acquired for the collection. A second canvas of a nude, in tones of ochre and brown, reveals Varley's fluent skill as a figure painter which sets him apart from most of the other Group members. His ability as a portrait painter is underlined by the dashing period piece, *Girl in Red*, a gift of Mrs. H. L. Rous, and by the lean, brilliantly executed *Negro Head* from the Charles S. Band bequest. The subtle blue and green landscape, *Moonlight at Lynn*, and a group of fine sketches and drawings round out the Varley selection. Outstanding among the drawings are a pen and ink mountain sketch and a penetrating study of an Indian girl.

Arthur Lismer was the Group of Seven's chief painter-biographer of the Georgian Bay District. His lush oil studies of the Bay area's vegetation and its pine etched island horizons compose the richest part of his life's work. Canada's foremost art educator, Lismer divided his time between teaching and creating. Summer after summer, he returned to Georgian Bay to search out the lichen-made patterns of its rocks and to track with brush and pen the tangle of its undergrowth. The canvas *Canadian Jungle* in the McMichael Collection is a key example of Lismer's interest in texture in nature. *Evening Silhouette* is his vision of the Bay islands at their most romantic. *Forest, Algoma,* painted further north, shows Lismer in a more reflective frame of mind, though no less monumental.

As the pictorial Boswell of the Group of Seven, Lismer created a large group of caricatures of his fellow artists during their meetings and sketching trips. Many of these rapid, witty commentaries round out the outstanding collection of Lismer works in the Kleinburg gallery.

Franklin Carmichael was the youngest of the founding members of the Group of Seven and his early death in 1945 removed one of the most appealing of its artists. Carmichael rarely attempted the big effect of overwhelming storm or blazing sunset. He was essentially a lyric painter engaged in capturing the tracery of new foliage or the passing of shadows across the backs of rolling forms of Lake Superior and the La Cloche Hills. There is a slight Oriental cast about many of Carmichael's oil sketches and watercolours, and there is a distilled and meditative air about them as though nature's forms were seen through the mirror of recollection. Almost all of the Carmichael works in the Collection possess his characteristic crisp sense of design. It is to be found equally in the large canvas *October Gold* and such small, carefully wrought panels as *Spring Garland,* and *Autumn Woods.*

A. J. Casson, a later member of the Group, was a protege of Carmichael. From his mentor, he learned discipline of design and fastidiousness of technique. To these, Casson added an interest in small Ontario villages that was peculiarly his own. Included among the examples by him in the McMichael Col-

lection are affectionate records of such communities as Norval, Kleinburg, Salem, Britt and Bancroft. Casson's large oil, *White Pine,* is as well known as any painting in the collection, made familiar to Canadians through a multitude of reproductions that hang upon the walls of offices, schools, banks and government buildings.

Two members of the Group of Seven are represented by several examples each. Frank Johnston is included with one tempera landscape and three oil sketches. Edwin Holgate's talents may be studied in a major figure study of the 1920's, *The Cellist,* and in three small oil studies of figures and landscapes. Group period paintings by both Johnston and Holgate are rare.

Two great Canadian landscape painters who, though not members of the Group of Seven, are well represented in the McMichael Collection are David Milne and Emily Carr. Contemporary with the Group in creative activity, both Milne and Carr were virtual recluses, preferring to cultivate their genius in isolation. Here the similarity ends, for a greater contrast of styles could hardly be found than that separating the paintings of Emily Carr and David Milne. Carr's art is a rushing, expressionist embrace of nature, full of exuberant swirling rhythms that suggest the lavish undergrowth of the Pacific Coast where she lived and painted. Milne's art is lean, and selective, reticent

at times almost to the point of sparseness.

The Milne canvases in the McMichael Collection are mostly from his New England period of the teens and 1920's. This was the time when Milne was given international honour by the inclusion of his work in the historic New York Armoury Show, which introduced modern art to America. That Milne's art is still worthy of international acclaim is borne out by the examples on view here. No artist in this country has surpassed the subtle tonalities and textures of such paintings as *Haystack*, *The Gully*, and *Mountains and Clouds*. Their seeming simplicity is the artfulness that results from long observation and intense concentration.

Emily Carr, as impulsive as Milne was reflective, is Canada's great expressionist painter. Her vast compositions seize the essentials of the British Columbia coastline and forests around which she spent her life. Noble in concept, irresistible in execution, her landscapes are overwhelming and eloquent confessions of her passion for her native land. Such works in the McMichael collection as *Reforestation*, *Shoreline*, *Swaying*, *Old Tree at Dark* and *Edge of the Forest* all testify to the genius of Canada's greatest woman artist.

Among artists recently introduced to the McMichael Conservation Collection are two of A. Y. Jackson's former painting companions, Albert Robinson and Randolph Hewton. Albert Robinson was unquestionably one of the most subtle and creative colorists Canadian art has known. He is represented at Kleinburg by the superb winterscape *St. Joseph, Quebec*, from the R. S. McLaughlin gift, and three characteristic sketches given by C. A. G. Matthews. The seven paintings by Randolph Hewton presented by Mr. and Mrs. Hugh Campbell suggest how much this gifted artist might have contributed to his country's painting had he continued in a full time career in art.

Quebec's favorite artist-sons share an honoured place at Kleinburg. Clarance Gagnon, J. W. Morrice and Maurice Cullen are all included in the collection.

Between 1967 and 1970, the size of both the McMichael Conservation Collection and the gallery itself, showed a dramatic growth.

In 1967, there were 287 paintings and drawings at Kleinburg; by 1970 these had increased to more than six hundred. This growth reflected the vastly increased support of the endeavor by other deeply interested Canadians. More than eighty percent of the new items were donated by private collectors.

In 1967-68, 8,000 square feet of floor space were added to the gallery. Another 21,000 square feet were built in 1969-70, bringing the total up to more than one acre of exhibition area. This increased size includes two of the most magnificent gallery rooms to be found anywhere in Canada, their ceilings reaching to a height of twenty-two feet. The walls stretch forty feet wide and eighty feet long. Such dimensions are ideal for hanging the major canvases of the country's landscape artists and the soaring roof line will easily accommodate a totem pole. One of these new galleries, in fact, was designed to house a totem pole, as well as other artifacts of the West Coast Indian culture and paintings of western themes. Here hang the monumental West Coast scenes by Emily Carr and Lawren Harris, along with views of the Skeena River area and the Rockies by such masters as A. Y. Jackson, J. E. H. MacDonald and F. H. Varley.

Western Canada, with its magnetic combination of visual atmospheric effects, possessed a great attraction for several members of the Group of Seven and for the great native woman genius, Emily Carr. Nowhere else in Canada can one find the dramatic combinations and contrasts of hard edged rock against soft, ephemeral mist. This challenging interplay of atmosphere and form brought out the best in the romantic nature of Fred Varley. His *Moonlight at Lynn*, with its ethereal character, is one of the most poetic pictures in the McMichael Conservation Collection. From the same Rocky mountains, Lawren Harris fetched forth a very different pictorial answer, in resolute, luminous compositions wrought with a razor-edged clarity. J. E. H. MacDonald had less success in some of his mountain studies than with his northern Ontario canvases, but when he did succeed, as in his *Goat Range* canvas, his efforts were as rewarding for us as any of the Group paintings of Western Canada.

Many of the finest treasures added to the McMichael Conservation Collection in recent years were donated by R. S. McLaughlin, who, in 1968, offered his entire collection of Canadian paintings to the Kleinburg gallery. This includes masterpieces by Clarence Gagnon, Maurice Cullen, J. W. Morrice and Emily Carr, along with many more by members of the Group. Among the outstanding individual works are J. E. H. MacDonald's *Forest Wilderness* and *Algoma Waterfall*, Emily Carr's *Old Tree at Dark*, Maurice Cullen's *Brook in Winter*, Lawren Harris' *Pic Island* and *Northern Lake*, A. Y. Jackson's *Radium Mine* and Arthur Lismer's *Bright Land*.

A very special gift from R. S. McLaughlin is a collection comprising the 54 small paintings created by Clarence Gagnon to illustrate a deluxe French edition of Louis Hemon's Maria Chapdelaine. These jewel-like studies, pristine in execution but astonishingly robust in color and form, have no equal in Canadian art. They stand alone for their complete authority in relating figures to landscape and in doing so with a warm humanistic emotion rare in our national painting. The completeness and dramatic impact of these Maria Chapdelaine paintings belie their small dimensions. Undoubtedly, they will take a favored place in the affections of many visitors to Kleinburg.

The collection's representation of works by A. Y. Jackson took a giant leap in the Autumn of 1968 when the late S. Walter Stewart donated his unequalled private collection of more than thirty Jackson paintings and sketches. Mr. Stewart was a life-long friend of the artist and had been a student at University when he bought his first panel by Jackson. The Stewart gift included six major canvases, as well as a delightful self-portrait of the artist as Pere Raquette (Father Snowshoes) as Jackson was sometimes called by the country folk of Quebec. Chronologically, the Stewart paintings cover every major period of the artist's career, from his early days in Europe to his visits to the Arctic and the Prairies. Among these is the original, on-the-spot, panel for the famous canvas, *The Red Maple* painted in 1914 on the Oxtongue River.

Many further contributions have come forward from other noted Canadian collectors during recent years. R. A. Laidlaw, who earlier had presented his priceless group of Tom Thomson and J. E. H. MacDonald sketches to the collection, continued to add major works and sketches by Tom Thomson, Lawren Harris, LeMoine FitzGerald and David Milne. The large Harris, *Mountains and Lake*, is one of his finest large compositions. FitzGerald's *Little Plant*, for all of its delicacy of style, must be considered among the half-dozen most important works by that fine Manitoba painter.

From Mr. and Mrs. C. A. G. Matthews came a collection which had been carefully put together over a period of many years. The sketches presented to the McMichael Conservation Collection include twenty-four fine examples by Arthur Lismer, Albert Robinson, J. E. H. MacDonald, A. Y. Jackson, Franklin Carmichael, A. J. Casson, Lawren Harris, Tom Thomson and J. W. Morrice.

Representation of the unique art of David Milne was much enhanced by bequests from the estates of the late Rt. Honourable Vincent Massey and Douglas Duncan. Mr. Massey bequeathed an oil, *The Stream*. Two others, including a version of Milne's most famous composition, *Painting Place*, came from the Duncan collection. The Duncan gift further enhanced the gallery with a large LeMoine FitzGerald work, *The Harvester*, and several watercolours by the same artist. Other important paintings were also presented by Drs. Samuel and Benjamin Raxlen, Mr. and Mrs. R. E. Dowsett, Mrs. Campbell Newman, Dr. and Mrs. Murray Speirs, the Honourable J. C. McRuer, Dr. Viola Pratt, Dr. Ian Urquhart and Mrs. Hugh Cameron.

Within any building in which art treasures are housed, safety is of paramount importance. Concern for the priceless and irreplaceable heritage which the Collection represents has caused its curator and Provincial authorities to design a thorough safety program. During the 1969-70 building program, Ontario Government experts installed a municipal-type system of hydrants to protect the building, and surrounding woodland. For safety and cleanliness, all the heat in the gallery buildings has been converted to electricity. During the day trained guides keep a polite, but watchful eye on all the gallery rooms. At night, the building is constantly patrolled by watchmen accompanied by dogs.

Preserving the unspoiled character of the land surrounding the McMichael Conservation grounds has been a prime concern of the authorities involved. Fortunately, some private owners of land in the area have been generous in sharing this concern with gifts of their own properties to the Province of Ontario. The late J. Grant Glassco and his family presented some 400 acres of land immediately adjoining the McMichael area to the Province. This gift ensures a broad area of conservation land for future public enjoyment along that picturesque stretch of the Humber River.

The beauty of its valley surroundings has also effected the design of the McMichael Conservation gallery. Throughout the construction of its rooms, great care has been taken to preserve a balance between solid gallery walls and windows which permit a view of the magnificent surrounding scenery. In this way,

the visitor is offered a frequent change of focus for his eyes, allowing them to rest on tree tops and hills between periods of close-up concentration upon the paintings.

No gallery of art should be judged on the merits of its physical structure and the quality of its contents alone. An important measure of the worth of any art institution is found in the efforts it makes to share its riches and in the success of those efforts.

Since its beginnings, the McMichael Conservation Collection has placed a strong emphasis upon reaching the widest possible public. This stress on the community and educational side of its existence, which originally was a very informal one, has now grown to a point where the Kleinburg gallery plays host to more than 1,000 school classes each year. As many as 2,000 people pass through its exhibition rooms in one day. On Mondays and Tuesdays, and the remaining weekday mornings, the galleries are reserved exclusively for the use of school children and cultural groups. Other afternoons and weekends are for the enjoyment of the general public. Even then, youth has shown a remarkable interest and gallery officials estimate that more than sixty percent of the general visitors are young people.

The gallery's educational program is now advised by a formal committee of prominent, professional educators. A full-time Educational Director arranges for all school visits and for the training of guides who tour the collection with students and other interested visitors.

The McMichael Conservation Collection by its very character lends itself to classroom extension studies. Thematically, it presents a panorama of the nation's geography. All parts of Canada are portrayed on its walls, from Newfoundland to Vancouver Island. There are characteristic views of the Maritimes, Quebec, Ontario and the Prairies. The Arctic tundra and the Polar seas are also well represented. Thus, the visiting student not only receives a vital introduction to Canadian painting but also gains a colorful lesson in the topography of his native land. For those interested in the legends and anthropology of

Canada's original settlers, there are the striking totems, masks and figures carved by our West Coast Indians and contemporary Eskimos, as well as pioneer artifacts.

The educational aspect of the McMichael Conservation Collection reaches out much further than school children. It includes the endless convention and cultural groups who often make a mass trip to the Kleinburg gallery as part of their plans. Thus, the collection reaches into all segments of Canadian life, from students to the retired Provincial Park guide who just wanted to renew his acquaintance with Algonquin.

Sometimes, the gallery personnel are faced with unexpected group visits such as the one that occurred in 1969 during an afternoon reserved for attendance by the general public. Towards closing time, a young woman appeared at the entrance to the gallery accompanied by more than forty children of elementary school age. She explained that she was a teacher and had brought her class by bus to see the collection. It was explained to her that school groups came only on certain days and mornings, and a reservation in advance was desireable because of the large number of applications. Furthermore, the educational guides had the afternoon off and it was closing time.

It was an unfortunate situation until, after some hesitation, the teacher explained that she and her students had driven down that day from Cobalt, 400 miles away—just to see the McMichael Conservation Collection! Such rare enthusiasm was rewarded by an immediate tour of the gallery, conducted by the Curator himself. The group was also introduced to A. Y. Jackson, for whom Cobalt had once been a favorite painting place.

"Do any of you", queried Jackson, "know a song called 'Cobalt is a Grand Old Town'? They used to sing it years ago when I was there."

Immediately, a forest of young hands was raised and, to please the famous artist, the school children serenaded him with a lively chorus of "Cobalt is a Grand Old Town". It is such incidents as this that make a gallery more than just another institution—and the teacher and her students from the northland undoubtedly went away thinking that the McMichael gallery was a "grand old place".

A. Y. Jackson himself unquestionably has been the grand old man of the McMichael Conservation Collection. He moved into a studio-apartment above the Kleinburg gallery late in June of 1968, while recovering from a serious illness. His presence has added much interest and color to the experience of many who come to Tapawingo. Jackson truly represents a legend in the flesh. He is history incarnate.

On the grounds of the McMichael gallery, three members of the Group of Seven are now buried. Under simple, large Algoma boulders, surrounded by evergreens, Arthur Lismer, F. H. Varley and Lawren Harris now rest in close proximity to many of the masterpieces they spent their lives creating.

For most visitors, the McMichael Conservation Collection represents much more than a gallery of fine pictures. It is a place that makes tangible the creative spirit of a whole people. From its beginnings as a small, private effort, the Kleinburg collection has grown to become an eloquent symbol of nationhood.

Tea Lake Dam. 1916
8½ x 10½

TOM THOMSON

Islands, Canoe Lake. 1915
8$^1/_2$ x 10$^1/_2$

Aura Lee Lake. 1915
8$^1/_2$ x 10$^1/_2$

Rushing Stream. 1915
8$^1/_2$ x 10$^1/_2$

The Phantom Tent. 1915-16
8$^1/_2$ x 10$^1/_2$

Spring Flood. 1915
8½ x 10½

TOM THOMSON 1877–1917

The life of Tom Thomson was the pure stuff of legends. Most of his later years were lived alone in the forest. His early death, & its mysterious circumstances, plus the meteor-like briefness of his dazzling career, combined to turn him into a national icon of art. In tribute to him, it would be difficult to improve on J. E. H. MacDonald's description of him, written for a memorial in Algonquin Park: "He lived humbly but passionately with the wild. It made him brother to all untamed things of nature. It drew him apart and revealed itself wonderfully to him. It sent him out from the woods only to show these revelations through his art. And it took him to itself at last."

Autumn Birches. 1916
8½ x 10½

TOM THOMSON

Moonlight, Canoe Lake. 1915
8¹/₂ x 10¹/₂

Moonlight and Birches. 1916-17
8¹/₂ x 10¹/₂

Afternoon Algonquin Park. 1914-15
25 x 32

Sunrise. 1916-17
8¹/₂ x 10¹/₂

Snow Shadows. 1915
8¹/₂ x 10¹/₂

Sombre Day. 1916
8¹/₂ x 10¹/₂

TOM THOMSON

Sunset. 1915-16
8½ x 10½

Log Jam. 1915
5 x 6¾

Smoke Lake. 1915
8½ x 10½

Black Spruce in Autumn. 1916
8¹/₂ x 10¹/₂

TOM THOMSON

TOM THOMSON

Rocks and Deep Water. 1916
8¹/₂ x 10¹/₂

Hoar Frost. 1915
8¹/₂ x 10¹/₂

Tamaracks. 1916
8¹/₂ x 10¹/₂

TOM THOMSON

Pine Island. 1914
8¹/₂ x 10¹/₂

Autumn, Algonquin. 1915
8¹/₂ x 10¹/₂

The Log Flume. 1915
8¹/₂ x 10¹/₂

Evening Clouds. 1915
8¹/₂ x 10¹/₂

Purple Hill. 1916
8½ x 10½

TOM THOMSON

TOM THOMSON

Beech Grove. 1915-16
8¹/₂ x 10¹/₂

Windy Day. 1916-17
8¹/₂ x 10¹/₂

New Life After Fire. 1914
8¹/₂ x 10¹/₂

Backwater. 1915
$8^1/_2$ x $10^1/_2$

Algonquin, October. 1915
$10^1/_2$ x $8^1/_2$

Summer Day. 1915-16
$8^1/_2$ x $10^1/_2$

Barns. 1926
8½ x 10½

A·Y·JACKSON 1882–

A·Y·Jackson has been more closely associated with the McMichael Conservation Collection than any other artist. A man of the earth, tanned & burnished by the elements he loved to paint, he has been an honoured artist in residence for several years. Kleinburg is the latest stop in a lifetime journey that has taken Jackson to every area of Canada. Over a career of more than six decades, he came to understand the geographic features of his country more intimately than any other man. He is undoubtedly the best known and most widely loved of all Canadian artists.

Sunlit Tapestry. 1939
28 x 36

First Snow, Algoma. 1920-21
42 x 50

Winter Morning, St. Tite Des Caps. 1934
21 x 26¹/₂

Village, Cape Breton. 1936
10¹/₂ x 13¹/₂

Church at St. Urbain. 1931
21 x 26

Eskimos and Tent. 1927
8¹/₂ x 10¹/₂

Grey Day, Laurentians. 1933
21 x 26

Indian Home. 1926
8¹/₂ x 10¹/₂

Valley of the Gouffre River. 1933
25½ x 32

Skeena Crossing. 1926
21 x 26

A. Y. JACKSON

Iceberg, at Godhaven. 1930
$8^{1}/_{2}$ x $10^{1}/_{2}$

Lake in the Hills. 1922
$24^{1}/_{2}$ x 32

Nellie Lake. 1933
31¹/₂ x 29¹/₂

Sand Dunes, Etaples, France. 1912
21½ x 25½

Cathedral at Ypres. 1917
8½ x 10½

Venice. 1908
8½ x 10½

October, Lake Superior. 1923
8½ x 10½

A. Y. JACKSON

Above Lake Superior. 1924
46 x 58

Superstition Island, Great Bear Lake. 1950
21 x 26

The Parlour. 1910
14 x 16

Houses, St. Urbain. c. 1934
8¹/₂ x 10¹/₂

A.Y. JACKSON.

Alberta Foothills. 1937
25 x 32

River, St. Urbain. 1930
8½ x 10½

Artist's Home and Orchard. 1927
8¹/₂ x 10¹/₂

J·E·H· MACDONALD 1873–1932
A quiet, gentle, poet-painter, J·E·H· MacDonald
gave as generously to his fellow painters as he did
to his own art. As mentor & counsellor, he helped to
guide and encourage the career of Tom Thomson,
as well as that of many other distinguished artists.
His own tapestry-like paintings weave together ex-
citing patterns of texture, colour and consummate
drawing. A master craftsman and designer,
MacDonald was incapable of making a sloppy or
careless creative gesture. The least of his sketches is
marked by a crisp refinement & sensitivity. The greatest of his canvases are sparkling masterpieces, un-
surpassed by any Canadian landscape artist.

Wheatfield, Thornhill. 1931
8¹/₂ x 10¹/₂

Algoma Waterfall. 1920
30 x 35

J. E. H. MacDONALD

Silver Swamp, Algoma. 1919
8¹/₂ x 10¹/₂

Northern Lights. 1916
8 x 10

Aurora. 1931
8¹/₂ x 10¹/₂

Forest Wilderness. 1921
48 x 60

J. E. H. MacDONALD

J. E. H. MacDONALD

Beaver Dam and Birches. 1919
8¹/₂ x 10¹/₂

Autumn, Algoma. 1918
8¹/₂ x 10¹/₂

Algoma Forest. 1920
8¹/₂ x 10¹/₂

J. E. H. MacDONALD

Wild Ducks. 1916
8 x 10

Lichen Covered Shale Slabs. 1930
8½ x 10½

Agawa Canyon. 1920
8½ x 10½

Young Maples, Algoma. 1920
8¹/₂ x 10¹/₂

J. E. H. MACDONALD

J. E. H. MACDONALD

Mountain Stream. 1928
8¹/₂ x 10¹/₂

Moose Lake, Algoma. 1919
8¹/₂ x 10¹/₂

Goat Range, Rocky Mountains. 1932
21 x 26

Algoma Reflections. 1919
10 x 13¼

LAWREN HARRIS 1885 – 1970

Lawren Harris was the theorist and intellectual of the Group of Seven · His endless creative curiosity led him into a more sophistocated search for new forms than any other Canadian painter · Starting from warm and relatively straightforward portrayals of buildings and people, he gradually redirected his talents over many years toward pure abstractions · He seems to have been most completely at home in those isolated areas of the country where forms are dramatically simplified – the north shore of Lake Superior, the Arctic Seas and the Rocky Mountains · In such places, he found a rarefied spirit which will always stir the vision of anyone concerned with Canadian art.

Early Houses. 1913
10 x 12

Mt. Lefroy. 1930
52¼ x 60⅜

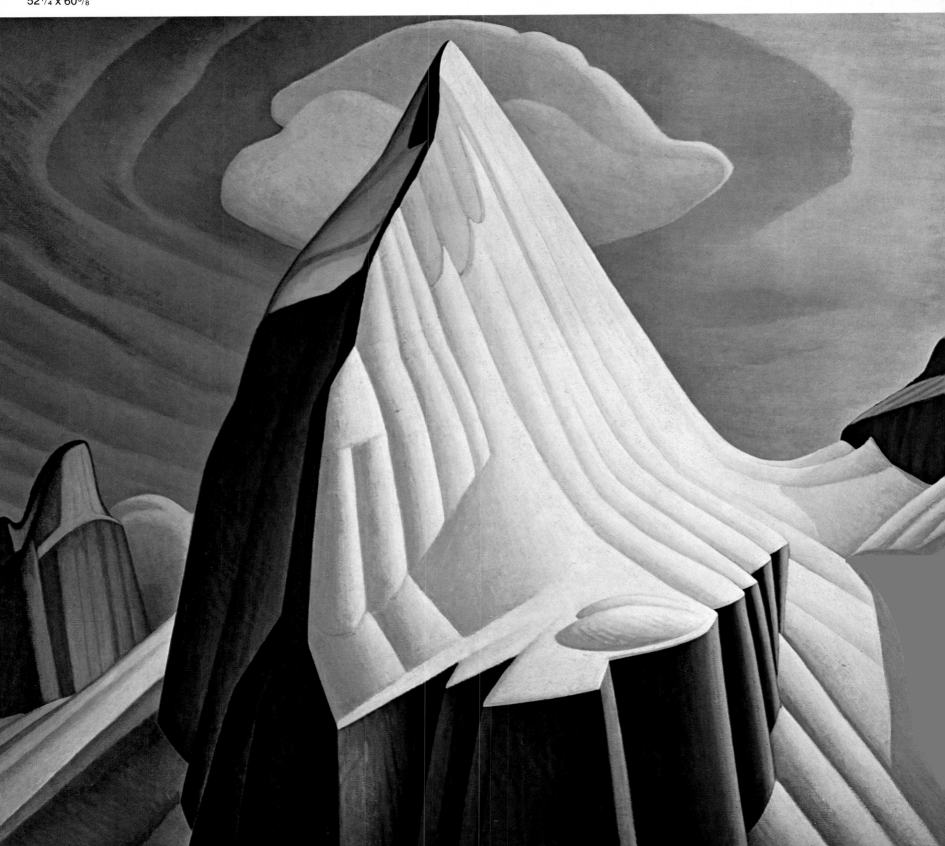

Northern Lake. c. 1923
32 x 40

Snow, Rocky Mountains. 1925
10¹/₂ x 13⁷/₈

Country North of Lake Superior. 1921
10¹/₄ x 13⁵/₈

Algoma Canyon. 1923
11³/₄ x 14⁵/₈

The Ice House. 1923
12 x 15

LAWREN HARRIS

Shimmering Water, Algonquin Park. 1922
32 x 40

Newfoundland Coast. 1921
10¹/₂ x 13⁵/₈

Mountains and Lake. 1929
$35^3/_4$ x $44^1/_2$

LAWREN HARRIS

LAWREN HARRIS

Eclipse Sound and Bylot Island. 1930
12 x 15

Ellesmere Island. 193[0]
12 x 15

Lake Superior Cliffs. 1921
11³/₄ x 14¹/₂

Algoma Woodland. 1919
10¹/₂ x 13⁵/₈

LAWREN HARRIS

Lake Superior Island. 1923
28 x 35

Castle Mountain. 1924
12 x 15

Montreal River. 1920
10½ x 13¾

LAWREN HARRIS

LAWREN HARRIS

South End of Maligne Lake. 1925
$10^{1}/_{4}$ x $13^{5}/_{8}$

Lake and Mountains. 1927
$11^{1}/_{2}$ x $14^{1}/_{2}$

Little House. 1911
$7^{3}/_{8}$ x $5^{1}/_{8}$

Pic Island. 1924
48 x 60

Stormy Sky, Georgian Bay. 1928
11³/₄ x 15⁵/₈

ARTHUR LISMER 1885–1969
Tall, gangly, endlessly cheerful, Arthur Lismer
possessed the keenest wit of the Group – and one
of its warmest spirits. His enthusiasm shows
throughout all of his paintings, with their dash=
ing style and bravura liveliness of texture. He
loved to paint the sparkle of light on water and
untidy foliage. He brightened up the Group's
outings by making brilliant, shorthand caricatures of their activities. His restless pencil and
Puck-like humor also won the hearts of those
thousands of young Canadians with whom he
came in contact as one of the world's foremost
art educators.

Dead Tree, Georgian Bay. 1926
12⁷/₈ x 16

Canadian Jungle. c. 1946
17¹/₂ x 22

ARTHUR LISMER

ARTHUR LISMER

Pine Wrack. 1939
21¹/₂ x 30

Rain in the North Country. 1920
8³/₄ x 12¹/₈

Lake Superior. 1927
12⁵/₈ x 15⁷/₈

Forest, Algoma. 1922
28 x 36

ARTHUR LISMER

Bright Land. 1938
32 x 40

Gusty Day. 1926
9 x 11⁷/₈

Evening Silhouette. 1926
12³/₄ x 16

ARTHUR LISMER

October on the North Shore. 1927
12½ x 15½

Near Amanda, Georgian Bay. 1947
11½ x 14¾

McGregor Bay. 1933
11 x 15½

Dead Tree, Garibaldi Park. c. 1928
12 x 15

F·H·VARLEY   1881 – 1969
Varley was the romantic of the group. His life
possessed the same will-of-the-wisp quality that
marks many of his poetic landscapes. He loved
Turner and his contemporaries and his work
confesses it. He valued colours for their mystic=
al qualities, blue, violet & green, he said, were
the spiritual hues and these are often dominant
in his pictures, even in his portraits. Until his
last years, he was constantly on the move, a
questing gypsy of the arts, always, it seems, in
search of the perfect landscape, the ideal model.

The Lions. c. 1931
12 x 15

Indians Crossing Georgian Bay. 1920
$11^{1}/_{2}$ x $15^{1}/_{2}$

Trees Against the Sky. 1934
$12^{1}/_{8}$ x 15

Arctic Waste. 1938
$8^{3}/_{4}$ x 12

Moonlight at Lynn. 1933
$23^{1}/_{2}$ x $29^{3}/_{4}$

Girl in Red. 1926
21 x 20³/₈

F. H. VARLEY

Portrait of a Man. 1950
27 x 18

Negro Head. 1940
15³/₄ x 11⁵/₈

Stormy Weather, Georgian Bay. 1920
8$^1/_2$ x 10$^1/_2$

Bolton Hills. c. 1922
9¾ x 12

FRANKLIN CARMICHÁEL 1890~1945

Franklin Carmichael was the most versatile member of the Group of Seven · He was equally at home working in oil, watercolour, wood engraving and commercial design · His pristine creations are invariably marked by superb craftsmanship · His shapes are always crisply delineated and his colour sparkling in its clarity · Carmichael favoured strong contrasts of light and shadow and cloud effects where his fine sense of design enjoyed full play · His deliberate approach to art fitted him ideally for teaching, a career he pursued at the Ontario College of Art for more than a decade.

Autumn, Orillia. 1926
9¾ x 12

October Gold. 1922
47 x 38¾

FRANKLIN CARMICHAEL

La Cloche Silhouette. 1939
10 x 12

La Cloche Panorama. 1939
10 x 12

Spring Garland. c. 1928
10 x 12

FRANKLIN CARMICHAEL

Indian Girl. 1932
30 x 24

YVONNE McKAGUE HOUSSER

Although she took her palette to many parts of the world, Yvonne Housser painted her most spirited works in the province of her birth · Countless Artists have visited the mining towns of Northern Ontario, but no one captured their special character more convincingly than she did in her canvases painted in the late twenties and early thirties · As a teacher and founding member of the Canadian Group of Painters she helped to continue the vitality of the Group of Seven forward in the painting of today·

Cobalt. 1928
10 3/8 x 13 3/8

Houses, Bancroft. 1955
11⅞ x 14⅞

A·J·CASSON 1898–

For the most part, A·J·Casson has left the more elemental and epic landscape of the northland to other members of the Group. His serene pictorial dramas have been played out mainly in southern and central Ontario. This may seem a restricted beat for art, but Casson has patrolled it faithfully over many decades with a keen and affectionate eye. He has been alert to make permanent for us the beauty of such mundane things as a rural storefront bright with signs, a farmhouse washday or the white triangle of a steeple wedged into a cobalt sky.

Old House, Parry Sound. 1932
9⅝ x 11⅜

Kleinburg, 1929
9¹/₂ x 11¹/₄

Flaming Autumn. 1936
10 x 12

A. J. CASSON

Sombre Land, Lake Superior. 1928
9 x 11

Rock and Sky. 1921
9³⁄₈ x 11¹⁄₄

Algoma. 1929
17 x 20

Drowned Land, Algoma. 1918
18 x 21

FRANK H·JOHNSTON 1888–1949

Frank Johnston's 1919–1920 paintings of Algoma are as compelling as almost anything by the Group done at that time. With a highly developed sense of the dramatic, Johnston would choose points of view, such as from an airplane which often gave it a very personal stamp. Johnston remained with the Group only briefly, afterwards concentrating on teaching and evolving a realistic manner of painting that made him one of the most popular artists of his area.

Moose Pond. 1918
10 x 13

Patterned Hillside. 1918
10 x 13

The Pool. 1965
8½ x 10½

EDWIN HOLGATE 1892–
F·H·Varley and Edwin Holgate were the Group's
two painters of people, but Holgate was the major
painter of the nude · His figure studies of the 1920's
and 1930's, with their backgrounds of the Canadian
northland, are the most monumental paintings of
their kind created in this country · Holgate's many
penetrating portraits represented a variety of sitters
from lumberjacks to the famed humorist, Stephen
Leacock · In his Laurentian and B·C· landscapes,
he reveals the same robust design that distinguish-
es all of his paintings ·

Melting Snow. 1948
8½ x 10½

The Cellist. 1923
51 x 38½

Nude. 1922
11½ x 10

Prairie. 1921
6½ x 8½

LIONEL LEMOINE FITZGERALD

Lionel LeMoine FitzGerald is the / 1890–1956
most famous painter of Canada's mid-west. His lean,
delicate studies of Winnipeg and the prairies turned
the commonplace of fields, barns and backyards into
compositions of almost ethereal beauty. At times,
particularly in his pen drawings, he flirted with pure
abstraction. Although he began as a neo-impression-
ist painter, FitzGerald pursued for most of his life
that crisp personal style which so clearly reflects the
lucid air and high skies of his Manitoba birthplace.

The Woods. 1929
9½ x 12

The Little Plant. 1947
24 x 18¹/₄

LIONEL LEMOINE FITZGERALD

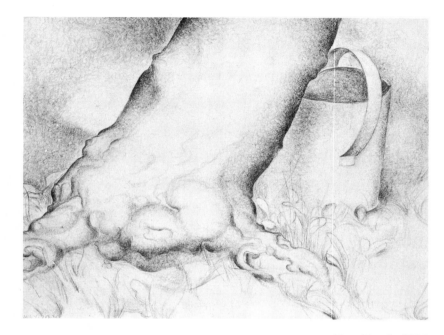

Tree Trunk. 1939
11¼ x 15

Williamson's House. 1933
60½ x 44

The Embrace. c. 1925
10½ x 12⅞

Clarke's House. 1923
12 x 16

DAVID B·MILNE 1882–1953

David Milne had perhaps the most personal style
of all Canadian painters of the first half of the 20th
century · From the richly encrusted early canvases
of the 1910 – 1916 period, through his dry brush
drawings of the 20's and the lean brown, ochre
and red still lifes and landscapes of the 30's and 40's,
he relentlessly pursued his own creative way · Milne's
economical style resulted from long experiment ·
He might paint a dozen different versions of the
same subject, each one revealing a slightly different stylistic approach and feeling · Eventually, he
distilled his theme down to the few washes & lines
which, for him, most intensely expressed a subject's
character ·

Clarke's House. 1923
12 x 16

Painting Place. 1930
11³/₄ x 15³/₄

DAVID B. MILNE

DAVID B. MILNE

Haystack. 1923
15³/₄ x 19³/₄

Blue Church. 1920
18³/₈ x 22⁵/₈

Patsy. 1914
20 x 23³/₄

Railway Station. c. 1929
12 x 16

DAVID B. MILNE

Pansies and Basket. c. 1947
14³/₄ x 21¹/₂

Boat Houses in Winter. 1926
16¹/₂ x 20¹/₄

Deer and Decanter. 1939
13³/₄ x 19

DAVID B. MILNE

DAVID B. MILNE

The Lilies. 1915
20 x 20

CLARENCE A·GAGNON 1881–1942

Clarence Gagnon was the pictorial bard of rural Quebec. The life and land of the habitant inspired him to some of the most engaging paintings ever made of the Canadian scene. His homage to his native province reached its most eloquent in a series of miniature masterpieces he created to illustrate the most famous of all habitant novels, Maria Chapdelaine. In these brilliant vignettes, Clarence Gagnon holds up a shining mirror for us to a now vanished peasant past.

Shoreline. 1936
27 x 44

EMILY CARR   1871 – 1945

From the forests of her native British Columbia,
Emily Carr created a unique art for the imaginat=
ion to dwell in and the eye to dwell upon · Living most
ly alone, she found ample company in her passion=
ate desire to proclaim in paint the movement of the
elements · Sea, sky, earth are joined by her work in
a swirling, rythmic whole · Her early interest in
the myths and totems of the west coast Indians de=
veloped later into a personal mysticism, in paint ·
By caravan, she travelled along the Pacific coast to
search out the shoreline, mountain or undergrowth
from which she wrought such powerful affirmations
of life .

Swaying. 1936
14 x 18

Reforestation. 1936
44 x 27

Edge of the Forest. c. 1938
33 x 22

On the St. Lawrence. 1914
8½ x 10½

ALBERT H·ROBINSON 1881–1956

Albert Robinson's studies of Quebec are among the most subtle line & colour compositions ever painted of the Canadian landscape· He built up his paintings with square, lozenge-like brush strokes and the resulting effect was almost of richly woven patterns· His favorite season was winter and his favorite theme French Canadian villages with their pastel tinted houses and horse-drawn sleds· Robinson's active career was all too brief; he painted very little in the last decades of his life when his hands were crippled from rheumatism·

Quebec Houses. c. 1920
8½ x 10½

Laurentians. 1914
8½ x 10½

St. Joseph. c. 1930
26 x 32¹/₂

ALBERT H. ROBINSON

Tunis. c. 1920-21
9 x 12½

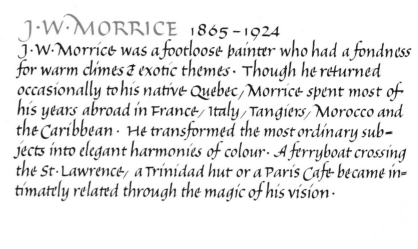

J·W·MORRICE 1865-1924
J·W·Morrice was a footloose painter who had a fondness for warm climes & exotic themes · Though he returned occasionally to his native Quebec, Morrice spent most of his years abroad in France, Italy, Tangiers, Morocco and the Caribbean · He transformed the most ordinary subjects into elegant harmonies of colour · A ferryboat crossing the St·Lawrence, a Trinidad hut or a Paris Café became intimately related through the magic of his vision ·

Algiers. c. 1919
10 x 9¼

Sailboat. c. 1911
4 x 6

Notre Dame. c. 1898
7¹/₂ x 9¹/₂

J. W. MORRICE

J. W. MORRICE

Cuba. c. 1915
10 x 12½

Along the Bank. 1908-10
4¾ x 6

Harbour. c. 1898
4¾ x 6

Clam Digging, France. c. 1914
4¾ x 6

Autumn Forest. mid 1930's
24 x 30

Slumber. mid 1930's
32 x 40

Benedicta. c. 1932
72 x 48

RANDOLPH HEWTON 1888–1960

Randolph Hewton had become one of Canada's most respected painters when he abandoned art for a business career in his early 40's. In his formative years, Hewton was closely associated with Albert Robinson and A.Y. Jackson, with whom he had been a fellow student under William Brymner.
His talent was especially strong in portraiture and figure painting.

Ontario

THE McMICHAEL CONSERVATION COLLECTION

CATALOGUE OF COLLECTION IN TOTAL   KLEINBURG • ONTARIO

All paintings, unless otherwise noted
are oil on canvas or panel.
All measurements are in inches.

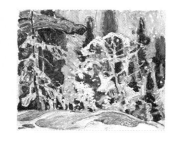

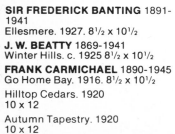

SIR FREDERICK BANTING 1891-1941
Ellesmere. 1927. 8½ x 10½

J. W. BEATTY 1869-1941
Winter Hills. c. 1925 8½ x 10½

FRANK CARMICHAEL 1890-1945
Go Home Bay. 1916. 8½ x 10½

Hilltop Cedars. 1920
10 x 12

Autumn Tapestry. 1920
10 x 12

October Gold. 1922
47 x 38¾

Autumn Woods. c.1922
9¾ x 12

Bolton Hills. c.1922
9¾ x 12

Dead Spruce. 1923
9¾ x 12

Tumbling Water. 1924
watercolour, 8½ x 10½

Scarlet Hilltop. c.1924
9¾ x 12

Northern Town. c.1931
10 x 12

Clouds and Sunburst. 1925
10 x 12

Autumn, Orillia. 1926
9¾ x 12

Elms. 1928
pencil, 8 x 10⅜

Spring Garland. c.1928
10 x 12

Old Store. 1930
watercolour, 3½ x 4¾

Farm House. 1930
pencil, 8 x 10⅜

Northern Tundra. 1931
30 x 36

Grace Lake. 1933
11 x 13

La Cloche Lake. 1934
pencil, 8 x 10⅜

La Cloche Mountain Tops. 1934
pencil, 8 x 10⅜

Cranberry Lake. 1934
pencil, 8 x 10⅜

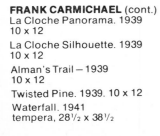

FRANK CARMICHAEL (cont.)
La Cloche Panorama. 1939
10 x 12

La Cloche Silhouette. 1939
10 x 12

Alman's Trail — 1939
10 x 12

Twisted Pine. 1939. 10 x 12

Waterfall. 1941
tempera, 28¹/₂ x 38¹/₂

EMILY CARR 1871-1945
Brittany, France. 1911
17³/₄ x 24

House and Garden. c.1912
15 x 18

Old Tree At Dark. c.1936
44 x 27

Reforestation. 1936
44 x 27

Swaying. 1936
14 x 18

Shoreline. 1936
27 x 44

Edge of the Forest. 1938
oil on paper, 33 x 22

Sand Dunes and Mountains. 1940
oil on paper, 21¹/₂ x 35¹/₄

A. J. CASSON 1898
Seated Nude. 1917
pencil, 8³/₄ x 5¹/₂

Nude, Back View. 1917
pencil and wash, 9 x 5⁵/₈

Nude Standing, Back View. 1917
pencil and wash, 9 x 5¹/₂

Trees. 1920
9¹/₄ x 11¹/₄

Rock and Sky. 1921
9³/₈ x 11¹/₄

Haliburton Woods. 1924
10 x 12

Poplars. 1925
10 x 12

Winter on the Don. 1926
watercolour, 17 x 20

Rocks and Clouds. 1926
linoleum block print, 8 x 8

A. J. CASSON (cont.)
Ice House, Port Caldwell. 1928
pencil, 7½ x 9¾

Nashville House. 1928
pencil, 8 x 10¼

Hillsburg. 1928
pencil, 7¾ x 10½

Country Store. 1928
pencil, 8 x 10¼

Galt Road. 1928
pencil, 7¾ x 10½

Sombreland, Lake Superior. 1928
9 x 11

Pike Lake. 1929
watercolour, 16½ x 20

Norval. 1929
10 x 12

Kleinburg. 1929
9½ x 11¼

Algoma. 1929
watercolour, 17 x 20

Pinegrove Village. 1929
watercolour, 9⅜ x 10¾

Farmhouse, Salem. 1929
pencil, 8 x 10½

Old Man in Rocker. c.1930
10 x 12

Spring Lasky. 1932
watercolour, 14 x 16

Old House, Parry Sound. 1932
9⅝ x 11⅜

Church and Graveyard. 1933
8½ x 10½

Millworker's Boarding House. 1935
9½ x 11¼

Old House. 1935
watercolour, 1¾ x 2½

Rapids and Rocks. 1935
9¼ x 11¼

Lake Baptiste. 1935
pencil, 7⅞ x 10½

Flaming Autumn. 1936
10 x 12

Algonquin Park. 1940
pencil, 6½ x 7½

Maple. 1941
pencil, 7¾ x 10½

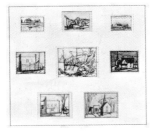

A. J. CASSON (cont.)
Fisherman's Point. 1943
tempera, 29¼ x 39¼

Lake of Two Rivers. 1944
9½ x 11¼

Picnic Island. 1948. 9½ x 11¼

Rocks and Waterfall. 1952
pencil, 5 x 6

Britt. 1955
pencil, 7⅛ x 7½

Houses, Bancroft. 1955
11⅞ x 14⅞

White Pine. 1957
30 x 40

Ontario Scenes. 1958/60
pencil, 15½ x 12

Tom Thomson's Shack. 1962
12¼ x 15

Mountains, Scotland. 1963
watercolour, 8¾ x 11⅞

MAURICE CULLEN 1866-1934
Brook in Winter. c.1927
24 x 32

LIONEL LEMOINE FITZGERALD
1890-1956 Trees in the Field. 1918
23⅞ x 22

Prairie Fence. 1921
6½ x 8½

Prairie. 1921
6½ x 8½

The Harvester. 1921
27 x 24½

Trees and Wildflowers. 1922
pastel
18¼ x 26

The Cupola. 1924
10½ x 10½

The Embrace. c. 1925
10½ x 12⅞

The Woods. 1929 Pencil
9½ x 12

Williamson's House. 1933
60½ x 44

Old Buildings and Shack. 1934
Pencil
14⅝ x 12¼

Geraniums and Trees. 1935
Pencil
12¼ x 8¼

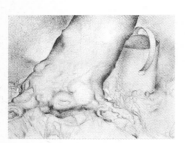

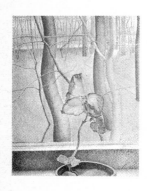

LIONEL LEMOINE FITZGERALD
Storm on Prairies. 1935
pencil
$8^{3}/_{4}$ x $11^{1}/_{4}$

Tree Trunk. 1939
pencil
$11^{1}/_{4}$ x 15

Cliffs. 1944
pastel 24 x 18

The Little Plant. 1947
24 x $18^{1}/_{4}$

Apple Basket. 1948
pen
$11^{7}/_{8}$ x $17^{7}/_{8}$

Trees. 1948
pen
11 x $7^{3}/_{4}$

Oak Bluff. 1950
watercolour
$10^{3}/_{4}$ x 15

Prairie Landscape. 1955
pen 9 x 18

CLARENCE A. GAGNON
1881-1942
Gagnon spent five years (1928-1933) lovingly portraying Quebec pioneer life in fifty-four superbly executed originals to illustrate Louis Hemon's Canadian classic ''Maria Chapdelaine''.

Mixed Media on Paper

C.G. 1	3 x $3^{1}/_{8}$
C.G. 2	$6^{1}/_{8}$ x 9
C.G. 3	$6^{3}/_{4}$ x $8^{1}/_{2}$
C.G. 4	$8^{1}/_{4}$ x $8^{3}/_{8}$
C.G. 5	$7^{1}/_{8}$ x $7^{1}/_{2}$
C.G. 6	$7^{1}/_{4}$ x 7
C.G. 7	$6^{3}/_{8}$ x $8^{3}/_{4}$

C.G. 8	$7^{7}/_{8}$ x $8^{7}/_{8}$
C.G. 9	$8^{3}/_{4}$ x $9^{1}/_{4}$
C.G. 10	$7^{3}/_{8}$ x $7^{3}/_{8}$
C.G. 11	7 x $9^{1}/_{2}$
C.G. 12	7 x $8^{1}/_{2}$
C.G. 13	8 x $7^{1}/_{4}$
C.G. 14	$7^{5}/_{8}$ x $8^{1}/_{8}$

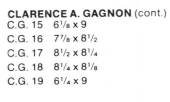  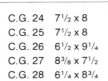

CLARENCE A. GAGNON (cont.)

C.G. 15 $6^{1}/_{8}$ x 9	C.G. 20 $8^{3}/_{8}$ x $8^{1}/_{8}$	C.G. 24 $7^{1}/_{2}$ x 8	C.G. 29 7 x $7^{7}/_{8}$	C.G. 33 $6^{7}/_{8}$ x 8
C.G. 16 $7^{7}/_{8}$ x $8^{1}/_{2}$	C.G. 21 $8^{3}/_{8}$ x 9	C.G. 25 $7^{1}/_{2}$ x 8	C.G. 30 $7^{5}/_{8}$ x $7^{1}/_{2}$	C.G. 34 $7^{1}/_{8}$ x $8^{1}/_{2}$
C.G. 17 $8^{1}/_{2}$ x $8^{1}/_{4}$	C.G. 22 7 x $7^{3}/_{4}$	C.G. 26 $6^{1}/_{2}$ x $9^{1}/_{4}$	C.G. 31 $7^{1}/_{2}$ x $8^{3}/_{4}$	C.G. 35 $6^{1}/_{4}$ x 9
C.G. 18 $8^{1}/_{4}$ x $8^{1}/_{8}$	C.G. 23 $6^{1}/_{8}$ x $8^{1}/_{2}$	C.G. 27 $8^{3}/_{8}$ x $7^{1}/_{2}$	C.G. 32 $6^{7}/_{8}$ x $9^{3}/_{4}$	C.G. 36 7 x $8^{1}/_{2}$
C.G. 19 $6^{1}/_{4}$ x 9		C.G. 28 $6^{1}/_{4}$ x $8^{3}/_{4}$		C.G. 37 $7^{3}/_{8}$ x $8^{1}/_{2}$

CLARENCE A. GAGNON (cont.)
C.G. 38   6¹/₄ x 9
C.G. 39   7⁷/₈ x 7⁵/₈
C.G. 40   6⁷/₈ x 9³/₈
C.G. 41   8 x 7⁵/₈

C.G. 42   8¹/₄ x 8
C.G. 43   6¹/₄ x 8¹/₂
C.G. 44   7⁷/₈ x 7¹/₂
C.G. 45   8 x 10³/₈

C.G. 46   7 x 7³/₄
C.G. 47   7³/₄ x 8³/₄
C.G. 48   7³/₄ x 8¹/₄
C.G. 49   7³/₄ x 8
C.G. 50   6³/₄ x 10¹/₄

C.G. 51   8³/₄ x 8³/₄
C.G. 52   8¹/₄ x 8¹/₄
C.G. 53   7³/₄ x 8¹/₄
C.G. 54   8³/₈ x 8³/₄

LAWREN HARRIS. 1885-1970
Rocky Brook. 1910
5⁵/₈ x 8³/₄

Old Mill. c.1911
10 x 8

Little House. 1911
7³/₈ x 5¹/₈

Laurentians. 1912
5¹/₂ x 8⁵/₈

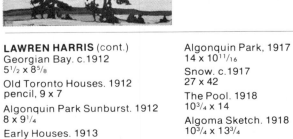

LAWREN HARRIS (cont.)

Georgian Bay. c.1912
$5^{1}/_{2}$ x $8^{5}/_{8}$

Old Toronto Houses. 1912
pencil, 9 x 7

Algonquin Park Sunburst. 1912
8 x $9^{1}/_{4}$

Early Houses. 1913
10 x 12

Lake Simcoe. 1916
$10^{1}/_{2}$ x $13^{3}/_{4}$

Algonquin Park, 1917
14 x $10^{11}/_{16}$

Snow. c.1917
27 x 42

The Pool. 1918
$10^{3}/_{4}$ x 14

Algoma Sketch. 1918
$10^{3}/_{4}$ x $13^{3}/_{4}$

Algoma Reflections. 1919
10 x $13^{1}/_{4}$

Algoma Woodland. 1919
$10^{1}/_{2}$ x $13^{5}/_{8}$

Beaver Dam. 1919
$10^{1}/_{2}$ x $13^{1}/_{2}$

Algoma Panorama. c. 1919
$10^{1}/_{2}$ x $13^{7}/_{8}$

Still Water, Algoma. 1919
$10^{1}/_{2}$ x $13^{1}/_{2}$

Montreal River. 1920
$10^{1}/_{2}$ x $13^{3}/_{4}$

Red Maples. 1920
$13^{1}/_{8}$ x $10^{1}/_{2}$

Portrait of Louise Julia Holden.
1921
$29^{1}/_{2}$ x 26

Early Houses with People. 1921
pencil, 8 x 10

Early Houses with Gatepost. 1921
pencil, 8 x 10

Newfoundland Coast. 1921
$10^{1}/_{2}$ x $13^{5}/_{8}$

Pic Island, Lake Superior. 1921
12 x 15

Lake Superior Cliffs. 1921
$11^{3}/_{4}$ x $14^{1}/_{2}$

Country North of Lake Superior.
1921
$10^{1}/_{4}$ x $13^{5}/_{8}$

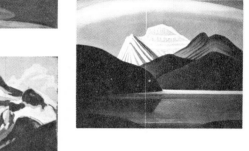

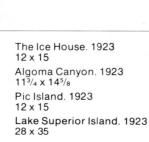
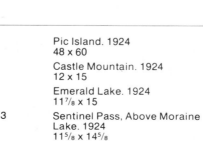

LAWREN HARRIS (cont.)
North East Lake Superior, 1921
$10^{1}/_{2}$ x $13^{5}/_{8}$

Northern Lake, Autumn. 1921
12 x 15

Shimmering Water, Algonquin
Park. 1922. 32 x 40

Northern Lake. c.1923
32 x 40

Pic Island. 1923
$11^{1}/_{2}$ x $14^{1}/_{4}$

The Ice House. 1923
12 x 15

Algoma Canyon. 1923
$11^{3}/_{4}$ x $14^{5}/_{8}$

Pic Island. 1923
12 x 15

Lake Superior Island. 1923
28 x 35

Pic Island. 1924
48 x 60

Castle Mountain. 1924
12 x 15

Emerald Lake. 1924
$11^{7}/_{8}$ x 15

Sentinel Pass, Above Moraine
Lake. 1924
$11^{5}/_{8}$ x $14^{5}/_{8}$

Emerald Lake. 1924
12 x 15

Mountain Sketch. 1924
12 x 15

South End of Maligne Lake. 1925
$10^{1}/_{4}$ x $13^{5}/_{8}$

Snow, Rocky Mountains. 1925
$10^{1}/_{2}$ x $13^{7}/_{8}$

Northern Lake. 1926
12 x 15

Lake and Mountains. 1927
$11^{1}/_{2}$ x $14^{1}/_{2}$

Mountains and Lake. 1929
$35^{3}/_{4}$ x $44^{1}/_{2}$

Eclipse Sound and Bylot Island.
1930
12 x 15

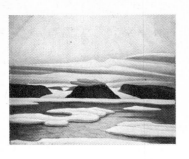

LAWREN HARRIS (cont.)
Ellesmere Island. 1930
12 x 15

Mt. Lefroy. 1930
52¼ x 60⅜

Maligne Lake. 1940
tempera, 30 x 40

RANDOLPH HEWTON 1888-1960
Apres-Midi Camaret. 1913
28 x 23

Benedicta. c.1932
72 x 48

The Purple Hill. Mid 1930's
20 x 24

Spring in the Valley. Mid 1930's
20 x 24

Autumn Forest. Mid 1930's
24 x 30

Slumber. Mid 1930's 32 x 40
EDWIN HOLGATE 1892-
Nude. 1922
11½ x 10

The Cellist. 1923
51 x 38½

Melting Snow. 1948
8½ x 10½

The Pool. 1965
8½ x 10½

A. Y. JACKSON 1882-
Elms and Wildflowers. 1902
watercolour, 10¾ x 13¼

Covered Bridge. 1906
12 x 17

Venice. 1908
8½ x 10½

Country Road, Bruges. 1908
7½ x 9½

Bruges, Belgium. 1908
7½ x 9½

The Parlour. 1910
14 x 16

Sand Dunes Etaples, France. 1912
21½ x 25½

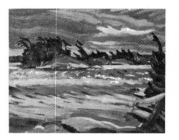

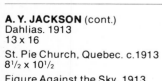

A. Y. JACKSON (cont.)
Dahlias. 1913
13 x 16

St. Pie Church, Quebec. c.1913
$8^{1}/_{2}$ x $10^{1}/_{2}$

Figure Against the Sky. 1913
$10^{1}/_{2}$ x $8^{1}/_{2}$

Algonquin Park River. 1914
$8^{1}/_{2}$ x $10^{1}/_{2}$

Algonquin Park Blue River with Rocks. 1914
$8^{1}/_{2}$ x $10^{1}/_{2}$

Riverbank and Green Trees. 1914
$8^{1}/_{2}$ x $10^{1}/_{2}$

The Red Maple. 1914
$8^{1}/_{2}$ x $10^{1}/_{2}$

Mount Robson. 1914
$8^{1}/_{2}$ x $10^{1}/_{2}$

Rapids. Algonquin Park. 1914
$8^{1}/_{2}$ x $10^{1}/_{2}$

Loretta Ridge. 1917
$8^{1}/_{2}$ x $10^{1}/_{2}$

Cathedral at Ypres. 1917
$8^{1}/_{2}$ x $10^{1}/_{2}$

Twisted Trees. 1919
$8^{1}/_{4}$ x $10^{1}/_{2}$

Beaver Pond in Autumn. 1919
$8^{1}/_{2}$ x $10^{1}/_{2}$

Beaver Lake, Algoma. 1919
$8^{1}/_{2}$ x $10^{1}/_{2}$

Agawa River. 1919
$8^{1}/_{2}$ x $10^{1}/_{2}$

Algoma Canyon. 1919
$10^{1}/_{2}$ x $8^{1}/_{2}$

Early Spring. 1920
$8^{1}/_{2}$ x $10^{1}/_{2}$

Storm, Georgian Bay. c/1920
$8^{1}/_{2}$ x $10^{1}/_{2}$

Go Home Bay. 1920
$8^{1}/_{2}$ x $10^{1}/_{2}$

Pere Raquette. 1921
tempera, 31 x 25

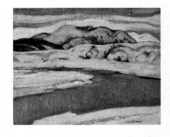

A. Y. JACKSON (cont.)
First Snow, Algoma. 1920-21
42 x 50

Waterfall, Algoma. 1921
8¹/₂ x 10¹/₂

Lake in the Hills. 1922
24¹/₂ x 32

Quebec Houses and Sleigh. 1923
8¹/₂ x 10¹/₂

October, Lake Superior. 1923
8¹/₂ x 10¹/₂

Murray Bay. c.1923
8¹/₂ x 10¹/₂

Above Lake Superior. 1924
46 x 58

Pic Island, Lake Superior. 1925
8¹/₂ x 10¹/₂

Barns. 1926
8¹/₂ x 10¹/₂

Totem Poles Indian Village. 1926
8¹/₂ x 10¹/₂

Indian Home. 1926
8¹/₂ x 10¹/₂

Skeena Crossing. 1926
21 x 26

Mt. Rocker Eboule near Hazelton,
B.C. 1927
8¹/₄ x 10¹/₂

Eskimos and Tent. 1927
8¹/₂ x 10¹/₂

Bic. 1927
8¹/₂ x 10¹/₂

Arctic Summer. 1927
pen, 6³/₄ x 6¹/₂

Labrador. 1927
pen, 7 x 6³/₈

Eskimo Summer Camp. 1927
20 x 25

Yellowknife Forest. 1928
8¹/₂ x 10¹/₂

Fishing Boats. c.1928
8¹/₂ x 10¹/₂

River, Baie St. Paul. 1928
8¹/₂ x 10¹/₂

Grey Day, Hull, Quebec. 1930
8¹/₂ x 10¹/₂

A. Y. JACKSON (cont.)
Ice Davis Strait. 1930
8¹/₂ x 10¹/₂

River Near Murray Bay. 1930
8¹/₂ x 10¹/₂

River St. Urbain. 1930
8³/₂ x 10¹/₂

Iceberg at Godhaven. 1930
8¹/₂ x 10¹/₂

Quebec Village. c.1930
8¹/₂ x 10¹/₂

St. Tite Des Caps. c.1930
8¹/₂ x 10¹/₂

Church at St. Urbain. 1931
21 x 26

Morning Les Eboulements. 1932
8¹/₂ x 10¹/₂

Cobalt. 1932
8¹/₂ x 10¹/₂

Blue Water, Georgian Bay. c.1932
8¹/₂ x 10¹/₂

Grey Day, Laurentians. 1933
21 x 26

Valley of the Gouffre River. 1933
25¹/₂ x 32

Quebec Village in Winter. 1933
8¹/₂ x 10¹/₂

Near Murray Bay. 1933
8¹/₂ x 10¹/₂

Nellie Lake. 1933
31¹/₂ x 29¹/₂

Les Eboulements. 1933
8¹/₂ x 10¹/₂

St. Lawrence at St. Fabien. 1933
8¹/₂ x 10¹/₂

Winter Morning, St. Tite Des Caps.
1934. 21 x 26¹/₂

Houses St. Urbain. c.1934
8¹/₂ x 10¹/₂

Algoma November. 1934
10³/₄ x 13³/₄

Cobalt Mine Shaft. 1935
8¹/₂ x 10¹/₂

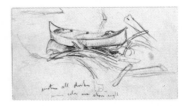

A. Y. JACKSON (cont.)
Village, Cape Breton. 1936
10¹/₂ x 13¹/₂

Alberta Foothills. 1937
25 x 32

Radium Mine. 1938
32 x 40

Sunlit Tapestry. 1939
28 x 36

Quebec Farm. c.1940
8¹/₂ x 10¹/₂

St. Pierre. 1942
8¹/₂ x 10¹/₂

St. Pierre, Montagne. 1942
8¹/₂ x 10¹/₂

Gaspe Near Pierre. 1942
10¹/₂ x 13¹/₂

Tom Thomson's Shack. c.1942
pencil, 8¹/₂ x 10¹/₂

Langlais Larch Sunshine Ski
Lodge. 1944. 10¹/₂ x 13¹/₂

Dog Ribb, Indian Chief's Grave.
1949. 21¹/₈ x 26¹/₈

Superstition Island, Great Bear
Lake. 1950
21 x 26
DRAWINGS — Pencil

Halifax, the Narrows Bedford
Basin. 1919. 6¹/₂ x 8¹/₄

Windy Day, Georgian Bay. 1920's

Quebec, seen from South Shore.
1922
7¹/₈ x 9³/₈

Ramparts in the Tonquin. 1924
8¹/₈ x 10¹/₂

Slate Isles, Lake Superior. 1925
9¹/₈ x 10³/₈

Canoe — Georgian Bay. 1925
4³/₁₆ x 7⁷/₁₆

Pines, Georgian Bay. 1925
8⁷/₁₆ x 11⁷/₁₆

Mt. Getsegyakla, Upper Skeena
River, B.C. 1926
7³/₄ x 9¹/₂

Potlatch Houses, Kispiox, Upper
Skeena River, B.C. 1926
7³/₄ x 9¹/₂

Hahao of Kitwanga. 1926
8³/₄ x 5¹/₂

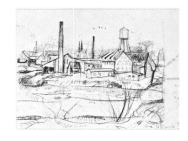

A. Y. JACKSON (cont.)
Mt. Rocher, Eboule, Hazelton, B.C.
1927
9 x 10¹/₂

South Coast of Bylot Island. 1927
7¹/₄ x 10⁵/₈

St. Simon. 1927
8¹/₂ x 11³/₈

Studies of Beothic and Eskimos.
1927
10¹/₂ x 7³/₄

Crap Game (Tutin, Dr. Livingstone).
1927
7¹/₂ x 9³/₄

Studies of Eskimos. 1927
7¹/₄ x 10⁷/₁₆

Yellowknife, Walsh Lake, Evening.
1928
9¹/₈ x 10³/₈

Fort Smith. 1928
7⁷/₈ x 10¹/₂

Crossing, Great Slave Lake. 1928
8¹/₈ x 10¹/₂

Fort Resolution. 1928
7³/₄ x 10¹/₂

The Beothic off Bache Peninsula.
1930
8¹/₂ x 11³/₈

Eskimo Tent at Pangnirtung. 1930
8⁵/₈ x 11¹/₂

On board the Beothic at Night. 1930
8³/₄ x 11⁵/₈

Coast at Les Eboulements, County
Charleboix. 1930
8¹/₄ x 10³/₈

Dead Tree Study. mid 1930's
6¹/₂ x 8¹/₄

Old Barn near Caledon, Ontario.
1930's
9 x 10³/₈

Old Mill, Cape Breton Island. 1930's
8⁵/₈ x 11¹/₂

Old Road, Northward from
St. Urbain. 1930's
7³/₄ x 10³/₈

St. Hyacinthe on the Yamaska
River. 1930's
8⁵/₈ x 11¹/₂

Church of St. Thomas, Frankville,
Ontario. 1932
8⁵/₈ x 11⁵/₈

Lake in Algoma East. 1933
8³/₄ x 11⁵/₈

A. Y. JACKSON (cont.)

Cobalt, Ontario. 1934
8½ x 11½

Thomson's Pt., Go Home Bay. 1934
8⅝ x 11½

Fishing Boats on Gaspe Shore.
1936. 8½ x 11⅝

Fox River, Gaspe. 1936
8½ x 11½

Fox River. 1936. 8½ x 11⅜

Blood Indian Reserve, Alberta. 1937
8⅝ x 11¼

Rain, McCallum's Veranda. 1937
8⅝ x 11⅝

Maynooth, Ontario. 1938
8¾ x 11¾

South from Great Bear Lake. 1938
8½ x 11⅜

Eldorado Mines, Echo Bay, Great
Bear Lake. 1938. 8½ x 11¼

Coastline of Great Bear Lake. 1938
8¾ x 11⅜

Bent Spruce, Great Bear Lake. 1938
8½ x 11¼

Grain Elevators, Western Canada.
1940. 8½ x 11⅜

Commissionaire Street, Montreal.
1940. 8½ x 11½

Street Scene on St. Tites des Caps,
Que. 1940's
8¼ x 11½

150 Mile House, B.C. 1940's
8⅜ x 11⅜

St. Pierre, County Montmagny,
Que. 1942
8½ x 11⅝

Canmore, Alberta. 1943
8⅝ x 11½

Old River Boats, Whitehorse,
Yukon. 1943. 8½ x 11½

Indian Village, Kamloops, B.C. 1943
8¾ x 11½

Farm Between Rosebud & Hwy.
518. 1944. 8½ x 11⅜

Miner's Shack, Barkerville. 1945
8¾ x 11½

Looking West from Harland's
Ranch. 1946. 8½ x 11¼

A. Y. JACKSON (cont.)
Indian Tents, Banff. 1946
$4^{11}/_{16}$ x $7^9/_{16}$

Hunter Bay, Great Bear Lake. 1951
$8^5/_8$ x $11^1/_4$

Yellowknife, N.W.T. 1951
$8^1/_2$ x $11^3/_8$

Houses above St. John's, Nfld. 1952
$8^5/_8$ x $11^5/_8$

Harbour of St. John's, Nfld. 1952
$8^1/_2$ x $11^1/_2$

FRANK H. JOHNSTON 1888-1949
Drowned Land, Algoma. 1918
tempera. 18 x 21

Moose Pond. 1918
10 x 13

Patterned Hillside. 1918
10 x 13

Dawn Silhouette. c. 1922
$4^1/_2$ x $6^3/_4$

ARTHUR LISMER. 1885-1969
J. E. H. MacDonald. 1912
pencil, $7^1/_8$ x $5^3/_4$

Tom Thomson at Grip. 1912
pencil, $7^3/_4$ x $8^3/_8$

Tom Thomson. 1912
brush and ink, 9 x 12

Tom Thomson's Camp. 1914
12 x 9

Maritime Village. 1919
12 x $14^1/_2$

Rain in the North Country. 1920
$8^3/_4$ x $12^1/_8$

Georgian Bay Islands. 1920
12 x $15^7/_8$

Gusty Day, Georgian Bay. 1920
9 x $11^7/_8$

Forest, Algoma. 1922
28 x 36

Knocker's Table. 1922
pencil, $18^1/_4$ x 30

Red Sapling. 1925
13 x 16

Evening Silhouette. 1926
$12^3/_4$ x 16

Dead Tree, Georgian Bay. 1926
$12^7/_8$ x 16

ARTHUR LISMER (cont.)
Old Barn, Quebec. 1926
11¼ x 15½

Lake Superior. 1927
12⅝ x 15⅞

Lake Superior Shoreline. 1927
12⅝ x 16

October on the North Shore. 1927
12¼ x 15½

Stormy Sky, Georgian Bay. 1928
11¾ x 15⅝

Pines Against the Sky. 1929
11¾ x 16

Moon River, Georgian Bay. 1931
12¼ x 15½

Pine and Rocks. 1933
12 x 15½

McGregor Bay. 1933
11 x 15½

Green Pool. 1935
12 x 16

Bright Land. 1938
32 x 40

Pine Wrack. 1939
watercolour, 21½ x 30

Mother and Child. 1946
12¼ x 9¼

Canadian Jungle. c. 1946
17½ x 22

Near Amanda, Georgian Bay, 1947
11½ x 14¾

Georgian Bay. 1947
11½ x 15½

Still Life with Greek Head. 1949
12 x 16

Pine and Rock, Georgian Bay. 1950
12 x 15⅞

Red Anchor. 1954
11⅞ x 15⅞

J. E. H. MACDONALD. 1873-1932
Nova Scotia. 1898
watercolour, 9⅜ x 4⅞

In High Park. 1908
3½ x 5

J. E. H. MACDONALD (cont.)
Oaks, October Morning. 1909
5 x 6⁷/₈

Snow, High Park. 1909
5 x 7

Chipmunk Point. 1911
7 x 5

Thomson's Rapids Magnetawan
River. 1912
6 x 9³/₁₆

Laurentian Storm. 1913
4¹/₂ x 4¹/₂

Elements, Laurentians. 1913
8 x 10

Snow, Algonquin Park. 1914
8 x 10

Gatineau River. 1914-15
8 x 10

Sunflower Garden. 1916
8 x 10

Near Minden. 1916
8¹/₂ x 10¹/₂

Wild Ducks. 1916
8 x 10

Northern Lights. 1916
8 x 10

Sunflower Study Tangled Garden
Sketch. 1916
10 x 8

Canoe Lake. 1917
8 x 10

Autumn Algoma. 1918
8¹/₂ x 10¹/₂

Moose Lake, Algoma. 1919
8¹/₂ x 10¹/₂

The Lake, Grey Day. 1918
8¹/₂ x 10¹/₂

Algoma Woodland. 1918
8¹/₂ x 10¹/₂

Rocky Stream, Algoma. 1918
8¹/₂ x 10¹/₂

Leaves in the Brook. 1918
panel, 8¹/₂ x 10¹/₂

Algoma Bush, September. 1919
8¹/₂ x 10¹/₂

Silver Swamp, Algoma. 1919
8¹/₂ x 10¹/₂

J. E. H. M٠CDONALD (cont.)
Beaver Dam and Birches. 1919
$8^7/_8 \times 10^7/_8$

Lake in the Valley. 1919
$8^1/_2 \times 10^1/_2$

Leaves in the Brook. 1919
canvas, 21 x 26

Stormy Weather, Algoma. 1919
$8^1/_2 \times 10^1/_2$

Agawa. 1920
$8^1/_2 \times 10^1/_2$

Algoma Trees. 1920
$8^1/_2 \times 10^1/_2$

Algoma Waterfall. 1920
30 x 35

Agawa River, Algoma. 1920
$8^1/_2 \times 10^1/_2$

Algoma Forest. 1920
$8^1/_2 \times 10^1/_2$

Algoma Hills. 1920
$8^1/_2 \times 10^1/_2$

Sungleams, Algoma Hilltop. 1920
$8^1/_2 \times 10^1/_2$

Tree Patterns. 1920
$8^1/_2 \times 10^1/_2$

Agawa Canyon. 1920
$8^1/_2 \times 10^1/_2$

Woodland Brook. 1920
$8^1/_2 \times 10^1/_2$

Young Maples, Algoma. 1920
$8^1/_2 \times 10^1/_2$

Forest Wilderness. 1921
48 x 60

Horses, Hardy's Barn, Oakwood.
1921
$8^1/_2 \times 10^1/_2$

Nova Scotia Barn. 1922
$4^1/_4 \times 5$

Nova Scotian Shore. 1922
$8^1/_2 \times 10^1/_2$

Buckwheat Field. 1923
$8^1/_2 \times 10^1/_2$

Pastures, Gull River. 1923
$8^1/_2 \times 10^1/_2$

J. E. H. MACDONALD (cont.)
Lake McArthur, Lake O'Hara Camp.
1924
$8^{1}/_{2}$ x $10^{1}/_{2}$

Valley from McArthur Lake, Rocky
Mountains. 1925
7 x 9

Cathedral Mountain. 1925
$8^{1}/_{2}$ x $10^{1}/_{2}$

Autumn Sunset. 1925
pen and ink, $8^{1}/_{2}$ x $10^{1}/_{2}$

Northern Pine. 1925
pen, $7^{3}/_{4}$ x $5^{3}/_{4}$

Lodge Interior, Lake O'Hara. 1925
$8^{1}/_{2}$ x $10^{1}/_{2}$

Prairie Sunrise. 1926
$8^{1}/_{2}$ x $10^{1}/_{2}$

Wiwaxy Peaks, Lake O'Hara. 1926
$8^{1}/_{2}$ x $10^{1}/_{2}$

Snow, Lake O'Hara. 1926
$8^{1}/_{2}$ x $10^{1}/_{2}$

Artists Home and Orchard. 1927
$8^{1}/_{2}$ x $10^{1}/_{2}$

Snow, Lake O'Hara Camp. 1927
$8^{1}/_{2}$ x $10^{1}/_{2}$

Cathedral Peak, Lake O'Hara. 1927
$8^{1}/_{2}$ x $10^{1}/_{2}$

Little Turtle Lake. 1927
$5^{1}/_{4}$ x $8^{1}/_{2}$

Mountain Stream. 1928
$8^{1}/_{2}$ x $10^{1}/_{2}$

Lake O'Hara, Rainy Weather. 1928
$8^{1}/_{2}$ x $10^{1}/_{2}$

Storm Clouds, Mountains. 1929
$8^{1}/_{2}$ x $10^{1}/_{2}$

Tamarack, Lake O'Hara. 1929
$8^{1}/_{2}$ x $10^{1}/_{2}$

Above Lake O'Hara. 1929
$8^{1}/_{2}$ x $10^{1}/_{2}$

Mountains and Larch. 1929
$8^{1}/_{2}$ x $10^{1}/_{2}$

Lichen Covered Shale Slabs. 1930
$8^{1}/_{2}$ x $10^{1}/_{2}$

Wheatfield, Thornhill. 1931
$8^{1}/_{2}$ x $10^{1}/_{2}$

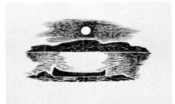

J. E. H. MACDONALD (cont.)
Aurora, Georgian Bay. 1931
8 1/2 x 10 1/2

Goat Range, Rocky Mountains.
1932
21 x 26

THOREAU MACDONALD. 1901-
Old House. c. 1924
mixed media, 5 1/2 x 7

Book Jacket. 1926
pen and ink, 7 x 6

Marsh Hawk. 1939
20 x 30

Great Horned Owl. c. 1940
23 x 24

St. John's, York Mills. 1940
pen and ink, 6 x 7

Squared Logs Near Purpleville.
1950
pen and ink, 5 1/2 x 6 7/8

Great Slave Lake. c. 1950
pen and ink, 9 x 12 1/2

Tom Thomson. 1965
pen and ink, 8 3/8 x 6 3/4

Man and Horse. 1965
pen and ink, 3 5/8 x 3 3/4

Man and Canoe. 1969
pen and ink, 4 x 8 1/2

Loon. 1969
ink drawing on paper 6 x 9

Canoe. 1969
ink drawing on paper 6 x 9

YVONNE McKAGUE.
(Yvonne McKague Housser)
1898-
Adriatic Docks. c. 1922
8 1/2 x 10 1/2

Houses in Valley. 1926
8 1/2 x 10 1/2

Cobalt. 1928
10 3/8 x 13 3/8

Quebec Village. 1928
24 x 30

Indian Girl. 1932
30 x 24

ISABEL MCLAUGHLIN
Mountains and Yellow Tree. 1964
19 x 15 1/2

DAVID B. MILNE. 1882-1953
West Saugerties. 1914
20 1/4 x 17

Relaxation. 1914
watercolour, 14 3/4 x 18

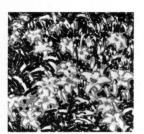

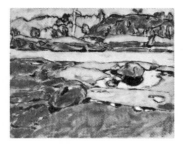

DAVID B. MILNE (cont.)
Patsy. 1914
20 x 23³/₄

The Lilies. 1915
20 x 20

Boston Corners. 1916
17³/₄ x 20¹/₂

The Gully. 1920
20 x 24

Blue Church. 1920
18³/₈ x 22⁵/₈

Clarke's House. 1923
12 x 16

Clarke's House. 1923
12 x 16

Haystack. 1923
15³/₄ x 19³/₄

Mountains and Clouds. 1925
15³/₄ x 19³/₄

Boat Houses in Winter. 1926
16¹/₂ x 20¹/₄

Floral Still Life. c. 1928
18¹/₄ x 26¹/₄

The Stream. c. 1928
16 x 22

Railway Station. c. 1929
12 x 16

Painting Place. 1930
11³/₄ x 15³/₄

Deer and Decanter. 1939
13³/₄ x 19

Forest Floor. c. 1943
13³/₄ x 20¹/₂

Pansies and Basket. c. 1947
14³/₄ x 21¹/₂

Canoe and Campfire. c.1947
13¹/₂ x 9³/₄

J. W. MORRICE.
1865-1924
Notre Dame. c. 1898. 7¹/₂ x 9¹/₂

Harbour. c. 1898
4³/₄ x 6

Sunset. c. 1898
4³/₄ x 6

Reflections. 1908-10
4³/₄ x 6

J.W. MORRICE (cont.)
In the Park. 1908 — 10
4³/₄ x 6

Winter in France. 1908-10
4³/₄ x 6

Along the Bank. 1908-10
4³/₄ x 6

Paris. 1908-10
4³/₄ x 6

The Promenade. 1908-10
4³/₄ x 6

Sailboat. c. 1911
4 x 6

Clam Digging, France. c. 1914
4³/₄ x 6

Roadside Scene. c. 1914
4³/₄ x 6

Cuba. 1915
10 x 12¹/₂

Village Square. c.1918
4³/₄ x 6

The Jetty. c. 1918
4³/₄ x 6

Algiers. c. 1919
10 x 9¹/₄

Tunis. 1920-21
9 x 12¹/₂

ALBERT H. ROBINSON. 1881-1956
On the St. Lawrence. 1914
8¹/₂ x 10¹/₂

Scene in Laurentians. 1914
8¹/₂ x 10¹/₂

Quebec Houses and Yards. c. 1920
8¹/₂ x 10¹/₂

St. Joseph. c. 1930
26 x 32¹/₂

TOM THOMSON. 1877-1917
Nearing the End. c. 1905
13³/₄ x 22³/₈

Young Fisherman. c. 1905
pen and ink, 12 x 18

Lady in Her Garden. 1906
17¹/₂ x 9¹/₂

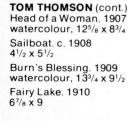

TOM THOMSON (cont.)
Head of a Woman. 1907
watercolour, 12⁵/₈ x 8³/₄

Sailboat. c. 1908
4¹/₂ x 5¹/₂

Burn's Blessing. 1909
watercolour, 13³/₄ x 9¹/₂

Fairy Lake. 1910
6⁷/₈ x 9

Red Forest. 1913
6⁷/₈ x 9³/₄

Springtime, Algonquin Park. 1913
6⁷/₈ x 9³/₄

Pine Stump and Rocks. 1913
6³/₄ x 9³/₄

Sunset Over Hills. 1913
7 x 9

Silver Birches. 1914
15¹/₂ x 22

Burned Over Land. 1914
8¹/₂ x 10¹/₂

Georgian Bay Islands #1.
1914
8¹/₂ x 10¹/₂

Georgian Bay Island With Pine #2.
1914
8¹/₂ x 10¹/₂

Pine Island. 1914
8¹/₂ x 10¹/₂

New Life After Fire. 1914
8¹/₂ x 10¹/₂

Afternoon Algonquin Park. 1915
25 x 32

Islands, Canoe Lake. 1915
8¹/₂ x 10¹/₂

The Log Flume. 1915
8¹/₂ x 10¹/₂

Log Jam. 1915
5 x 6³/₄

Evening Clouds. 1915
8¹/₂ x 10¹/₂

Autumn Algonquin. 1915
8¹/₂ x 10¹/₂

Autumn Clouds. 1915
8¹/₂ x 10¹/₂

TOM THOMSON (cont.)
Spring Flood. 1915
8¹/₂ x 10¹/₂

Algonquin, October. 1915
10¹/₂ x 8¹/₂

Burned Over Swamp. 1915
8¹/₂ x 10¹/₂

Poplar Hillside. 1915
8¹/₂ x 10¹/₂

Smoke Lake. 1915
8¹/₂ x 10¹/₂

Moonlight, Canoe Lake. 1915
8¹/₂ x 10¹/₂

Deer. 1915
pencil, 4³/₄ x 7¹/₂

Deer. 1915
pencil, 4³/₄ x 7¹/₂

Deer. 1915
pencil, 4³/₄ x 7¹/₂

Backwater. 1915
8¹/₂ x 10¹/₂

Aura Lee Lake. 1915
8¹/₂ x 10¹/₂

Rushing Stream. 1915
8¹/₂ x 10¹/₂

Hoar Frost. 1915
8¹/₂ x 10¹/₂

Snow Shadows. 1915
8¹/₂ x 10¹/₂

Beech Grove. 1915/16
8¹/₂ x 10¹/₂

Sunset. 1915/16
8¹/₂ x 10¹/₂

Wood Interior. 1915/16
8¹/₂ x 10¹/₂

Lake, Hills and Sky. 1915/16
8¹/₂ x 10¹/₂

Summer Day. 1915/16
8¹/₂ x 10¹/₂

Phantom Tent. 1915/16
8¹/₂ x 10¹/₂

TOM THOMSON (cont.)
Autumn Colour. 1916
8¹/₂ x 10¹/₂
Autumn Birches. 1916
8¹/₂ x 10¹/₂
Rocks and Deep Water. 1916
8¹/₂ x 10¹/₂
Sombre Day. 1916
8¹/₂ x 10¹/₂

Black Spruce in Autumn. 1916
8¹/₂ x 10¹/₂
Purple Hill. 1916
8¹/₂ x 10¹/₂
Tea Lake Dam. 1916
8¹/₂ x 10¹/₂
Tamaracks. 1916
8¹/₂ x 10¹/₂

Ragged Pine. 1916
8¹/₂ x 10¹/₂
Moonlight and Birches. 1916/17
8¹/₂ x 10¹/₂
Sunrise. 1916-17
8¹/₂ x 10¹/₂
Windy Day. 1916/17
8¹/₂ x 10¹/₂

F. H. VARLEY 1881-1969
Indians Crossing Georgian Bay.
1920
11¹/₂ x 15¹/₄
Nude. c. 1920
24 x 16
Stormy Weather, Georgian Bay.
1920
8¹/₂ x 10¹/₂
Little Girl. 1923
11¹/₂ x 15

Meadowvale. 1923
8 x 10
John in the Studio. 1924
pen and ink, 10¹/₂ x 8¹/₂
Mountain Portage. 1925
20 x 24
Girl in Red. 1926
21 x 20³/₈

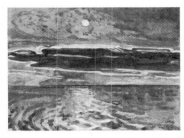

F. H. VARLEY (cont.)
Mountains. 1927
pen and ink, 12 x 14

Indian Girl. 1927
mixed media, 8$^{7}/_{8}$ x 7$^{7}/_{8}$

Sketchers. 1927
pencil, 12 x 14$^{3}/_{4}$

Dead Tree, Garibaldi Park. c. 1928
12 x 15

Blue Pool. 1930
11 x 13

The Lions. c. 1931
12 x 15

Moonlight at Lynn. 1933
23$^{1}/_{2}$ x 29$^{3}/_{4}$

West Coast Inlet. c. 1933
12 x 14$^{7}/_{8}$

Trees Against the Sky. 1934
12$^{1}/_{8}$ x 15

Arctic Waste. 1938
watercolour, 8$^{3}/_{4}$ x 12

Iceberg. 1938
12 x 15

Eskimo Woman. 1938
mixed media, 9 x 3$^{1}/_{2}$

Negro Head. 1940
15$^{3}/_{4}$ x 11$^{5}/_{8}$

Portrait of Doctor Mason. c. 1940
mixed media, 14 x 10

Portrait of Old Man. c. 1942
charcoal, 16$^{1}/_{2}$ x 12$^{7}/_{8}$

Hilltop Doon. 1948
11$^{3}/_{4}$ x 15

Fall Landscape. 1948
12 x 15

Portrait of a Man. 1950
27 x 18

Little Lake, Bras D'Or. 1953
9$^{1}/_{2}$ x 12

Pine Tree. c. 1959
mixed media, 12 x 8$^{7}/_{8}$

Designed by A. J. Casson, LL.D., R.C.A.
Photography Hugh W. Thompson
Produced by Sampson Matthews Limited, Toronto